Project Report 77

London, 2000

Prop loads in large braced excavations

W Powrie

M Batten

**Books are to be returned on or before
the last date below.**

LIBREX —

CIRIA *sharing knowledge ∎ building best practice*

6 Storey's Gate, Westminster, London SW1P 3AU
TELEPHONE 0207 222 8891   FAX 0207 222 1708
EMAIL enquiries@ciria.org.uk
WEBSITE www.ciria.org.uk

Prop loads in large braced excavations

Powrie, W and Batten, M

Construction Industry Research and Information Association

Project Report 77   © CIRIA 2000   ISBN 0 86017 877 3

Keywords		
Case histories, *in-situ* measurements, instrumentation numerical analyses, prop loads, structural considerations, temperature effects, temporary props, vibrating wire strain gauges		

Reader interest	Classification	
Temporary works designers, geotechnical engineers, project managers	AVAILABILITY	Unrestricted
	CONTENT	Guidance based on review and current practice
	STATUS	Committee-guided
	USER	Civil and structural engineers

Summary

Embedded walls retaining the sides of large excavations are often supported at some stage in the construction process by temporary props at one or more levels, in order to reduce wall and ground movements. The provision of temporary props, which typically consist of tubular steel sections 1 m or more in diameter, is costly in terms of money and time. There may also be risk to the site operatives involved in installing and removing them. The advantages of reducing the number of temporary props or eliminating some levels of propping in a large excavation are therefore considerable.

There is a widely held view within the construction industry that the procedures currently used in design tend to overestimate actual prop loads. The main aim of the research was to investigate the reasons for this apparent discrepancy by monitoring and analysing the temporary prop loads developed during construction of the London Underground Jubilee Line Extension stations at Canada Water and Canary Wharf. Prop temperatures were also measured to assess their influence on prop loads.

For the stiff, reinforced concrete walls at Canada Water and Canary Wharf, the research showed that:

1. Temporary prop loads, calculated using limit equilibrium and finite element analysis, were similar to those measured in the field (neglecting temperature effects) provided that appropriate soil parameters and input assumptions were used. In finite element analyses, key factors were the effect of wall installation and the timescale of excess pore water pressure dissipation in low-permeability strata. In limit equilibrium analyses, realistic prop loads were calculated on the basis of fully active conditions in the retained soil. Although in design a margin of safety is essential to allow for events such as the accidental removal of a prop, the over-prediction of prop loads seems to result from a consistently conservative set of design assumptions, rather than any flaw in the underlying soil mechanics principles.

2. Temperature-induced axial loads accounted for up to 40 per cent of the total load carried by a prop installed at a low temperature. Temperature-induced axial loads, in principle, may be estimated from the anticipated temperature rise, the coefficient of thermal expansion of the prop, and the degree of end restraint provided by the wall and the soil behind it. At Canada Water and Canary Wharf the degree of end restraint for props near the crest was ~50 per cent. For the low-level props at Canada Water the degree of end restraint was ~65 per cent.

3. In the absence of non-uniformities from lack of fit at the ends of a prop, bending moments resulting from wall rotation and/or temperature gradients across the prop should be expected to be of the same order as those due to self-weight effects. However, a lack of fit between the walings and the ends of a prop could increase secondary bending effects substantially – a point that may need to be considered in design.

4. Vibrating wire strain gauges are entirely suitable for measuring temporary prop loads, provided that certain basic guidelines are followed.

Foreword

The research that is the subject of this report was sponsored by the Engineering and Physical Sciences Research Council (EPSRC), under Grant Reference GR/55974. As a condition of EPSRC grants, the researchers are required to submit a final report summarising the work done, the principal findings and, where appropriate, their relevance to engineering practice. This research was collaborative, based on two sites of the Jubilee Line Extension project and involving a steering group from industry. The report, which has been reviewed and accepted by EPSRC as the research funder, has also been reviewed by representatives of the collaborating partners, who guided the project work as steering group members. CIRIA, as a collaborating organisation, undertook to issue the final report to CIRIA Core members as part of the process of disseminating the results of the research and as part of CIRIA's research project "Prop loads: guidance on design".

The research was carried out by Melanie Batten, who was based on site at Canada Water and Canary Wharf for the first 18 months of the project. Ms Batten was employed by the University of Southampton as a research assistant, and was later awarded the degree of PhD. The project was supervised by Professor William Powrie of the University of Southampton, and overseen by a steering group comprising the following industry representatives:

E C Chaplin (chairman)	(then of) Tarmac Construction Limited
D R Beadman	Bachy Group
R Boorman	(then of) Wimpey Construction Limited
J Henderson	Tarmac Construction Limited (Canary Wharf site to December 1995)
Q J Leiper	Tarmac Construction Limited
R McGivern	Wimpey Construction Limited (Canada Water site)
D Roberts	Tarmac Construction Limited (Canary Wharf site from January 1996)
Dr M R Sansom	CIRIA
D Twine	Ove Arup and Partners
Dr H-T Yu	(then of) Trafalgar House Technology

In addition, the draft of this report was reviewed by steering group members of CIRIA's research project RP526. CIRIA's research managers were Dr M R Sansom and F M Jardine.

ACKNOWLEDGEMENTS

CIRIA and the authors gratefully acknowledge EPSRC for permission to publish this report and for funding the research on which it is based; Construction Directorate of the Department of the Environment, Transport and the Regions and CIRIA's Core Programme for funding Research Project RP526, and thereby the preparation of this report; Tarmac Construction, Wimpey Construction, Bachy (UK) Limited (now Bachy Soletanche) and Trafalgar House Technology (now Kvaerner Technology) who collaborated in the research; their staff on the Canada Water and Canary Wharf station construction sites; and London Underground Limited whose Jubilee Line Extension Project sites these were.

Contents

TABLES

FIGURES

1 Background and objectives

1.1 BACKGROUND

Embedded walls retaining the sides of large excavations are often supported at some stage in the construction process by temporary props at one or more levels, in order to reduce wall and ground movements. The provision of these temporary props, which are typically tubular steel sections 1 m or more in diameter, is costly in terms of both money and time. There is also an element of risk for the site operatives involved in installing and removing the props. The potential advantages of reducing the number of temporary props and/or eliminating some levels of propping in a large excavation are therefore considerable.

Temporary props are usually designed and specified based on some form of analysis. There is a widely held view within the construction industry (eg Glass and Powderham, 1994; Marchand, 1997) that the procedures used tend to overestimate actual prop loads. Research carried out during the early 1990s highlighted some of the possible reasons for this. They included the reduction in lateral stress from the *in-situ* condition during wall installation; the high stiffness of the retained soil in the stress path followed during excavation in front of the wall; three-dimensional and groundwater level effects; and the timescale of pore water pressure equilibration following construction. The construction of the London Underground Jubilee Line Extension (JLE) stations at Canada Water and Canary Wharf between 1994 and 1997, in open excavations supported by *in-situ* concrete retaining walls, offered a unique and timely opportunity to investigate the significance of these effects in practice.

1.2 AIMS AND OBJECTIVES

The main aim of the research was to investigate the apparent discrepancy between measured prop loads and those allowed for in design, by monitoring and analysis of the temporary prop loads developed during the construction of the Jubilee Line Extension stations at Canada Water and Canary Wharf. Prop temperatures were also measured to assess the influence of temperature changes on the prop loads.

The specific objectives were:

- to monitor temporary prop loads, temperatures, pore water pressures and wall movements during construction of two stations on the Jubilee Line Extension
- to compare the measured prop loads and wall movements with those calculated using conventional methods of design and state-of the-art back-analyses
- to investigate and identify the reasons for any discrepancies between measured and calculated prop loads.

It was intended that the results of the project should lead to the development of more reliable design methods for temporary props, leading to a reduction in both costs and risk to site operatives.

2   Description of the research

The research involved monitoring and analysis of temporary prop loads during construction of the Jubilee Line Extension stations at Canada Water and Canary Wharf, with particular reference to the assumptions and methods typically used in design. Additional information used in the interpretation of the prop loads included comprehensive site investigation data, inclinometer and piezometer readings, fabrication details of the props and their support systems, and diaries of excavation and construction events. This section describes the instrumentation and methods of analysis used, and gives details of the two sites.

2.1   CANADA WATER: SITE AND EXCAVATION GEOMETRY

2.1.1   Ground conditions

There are six soil types present at Canada Water (Figure 2.1), the main geotechnical parameters of which are summarised in Table 2.1. These have been derived primarily from the results of *in-situ* and laboratory tests presented in the interpretative report associated with the JLE site investigation (Geotechnical Consulting Group, 1991). As indicated, there is a wide range of possible values for the soil permeabilities (k) and stiffnesses (Young's moduli, E'). The Woolwich Clays and Woolwich Sands referred to in this report are beds of the Lambeth Group.

Table 2.1   *Geotechnical parameters for soils at Canada Water*

Soil type	Level at top of stratum (m TD[†])	ρ (kg/m³)	ϕ'_{peak} (°)	ϕ'_{crit} (°)	E' (MN/m²)	k (m/s)	K_0
Made ground	105.5	1800	40	25	2–20	3.6×10^{-5}–1.6×10^{-3}	0.5
Alluvium	99.5	1850	28	25	2	1×10^{-8}–1×10^{-5}	0.8
Thames Gravels	98	2000	38	35	15–90	1×10^{-4}–1×10^{-3}	0.5
Woolwich Clays of Lambeth Group	94	2200	30	27	30–110	1.2×10^{-7}–1.3×10^{-5} (h)[#] 1×10^{-12}–1×10^{-10} (v)[#]	1.5
Woolwich Sands of Lambeth Group	90	2200	34	30	100–310	2.8×10^{-7}–2.8×10^{-5} (h)[#] 1×10^{-8}–2.8×10^{-7} (v)[#]	1.5
Thanet Beds	84	2200	47	33	300–450[*]	1.9–2.3×10^{-5}	1.0

[†]   All levels are expressed relative to the Tunnel Datum, TD, which is 100 m below Ordnance Datum

[*]   Stiffness of the Thanet Beds increases linearly from the minimum at the top of the stratum to the maximum at the base of the stratum.

[#]   (h) and (v) indicate permeabilities in the horizontal and vertical directions respectively.

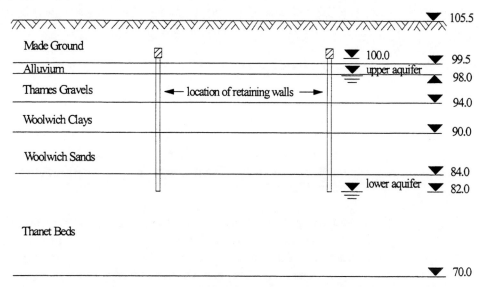

Figure 2.1 *Ground conditions showing approximate groundwater levels during the construction of Canada Water station*

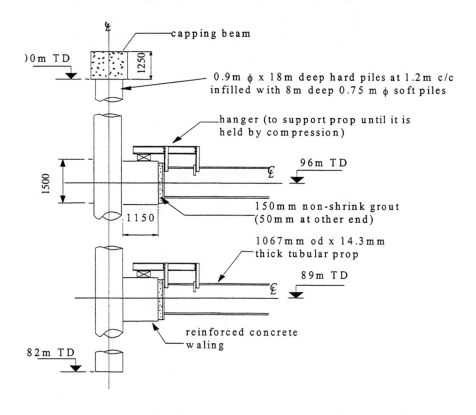

Figure 2.2 *Prop end details: Canada Water*

2.1.2 Groundwater conditions

There are two aquifers at the site: a shallow aquifer comprising the Alluvium and the Thames Gravels, which lie above the relatively impermeable Lambeth Group clays (Woolwich Clays); and a deep aquifer comprising the Lambeth Group (Woolwich) Sands, the Thanet Beds and the Upper Chalk. During the construction period the piezometric level in the upper aquifer, within which pore water pressures were hydrostatic, was approximately 98 m TD. The groundwater level in the lower aquifer was lowered to beneath the toe of the wall (82 m TD) during construction of the station to stabilise the base of the excavation. Although no data are available, it is likely that the pore water pressures in the Woolwich Clays fell gradually towards zero at the base of this relatively impermeable stratum.

2.1.3 Construction details

The station was built in an excavation approximately 150 m long and 26.7 m wide, the sides of which were supported during construction by 18 m deep contiguous pile retaining walls. In the research area, the excavation was approximately 17 m deep and the wall was supported at two levels by 1067 mm diameter × 14.3 mm thick tubular steel props at 8.3 m centres. The props spanned 24.1 m between continuous concrete waling beams (Figure 2.2).

Four props were monitored: two at elevation 96 m TD (props U1 and U2) and two at elevation 89 m TD (prop L1, which was below prop U1 and prop L2, which was below prop U2). The top of the wall was at 100 m TD, approximately 5.5 m below original ground level. The hard piles were 18 m deep, giving a toe level of 82 m TD. Over the upper part of the wall these were infilled with 8 m deep secant soft piles, which extended 2 m below the top of the Woolwich Clays to prevent the ingress of water from the upper aquifer. The construction sequence is given in Table 2.3.

2.2 CANARY WHARF: SITE AND EXCAVATION GEOMETRY

2.2.1 Ground conditions

The soil types at Canary Wharf are shown on Figure 2.3. For Canada Water, the soil parameters have, where possible, been derived from the *in-situ* and laboratory testing carried out as part of the site investigation (Ove Arup and Partners, 1991). The geotechnical parameters for each soil type are summarised in Table 2.2.

Table 2.2 *Geotechnical parameters for soils at Canary Wharf*

Soil type	Level at top of stratum (m TD[†])	ρ (kg/m³)	ϕ'_{peak} (°)	ϕ'_{crit} (°)	E' (MN/m²)	k (m/s)	K_0
Dock silt	96.5	1950	n/a	n/a	1	1×10^{-4}	0.5
Thames Gravels	95	2000	36	35	15–75	5×10^{-4}–1.5×10^{-3}	0.5
Woolwich Clays	92	2100	27	24	35–60[*]	1.2×10^{-7}–1.3×10^{-5} (h)[#] 1×10^{-12}–1×10^{-10} (v)[#]	2.3
Woolwich Sands	87	2100	33	28	100–230	2.8×10^{-7}–2.8×10^{-5} (h)[#] 1×10^{-8}–1×10^{-7} (v)[#]	1
Thanet Beds	84	2100	40	33	180–210 (h)[#] 250–500 (v)[#]	3×10^{-5}–1×10^{-4}	1.1
Chalk	68	2000	–	39	200–560[*]	9×10^{-5}	1

[†] All levels are expressed relative to the Tunnel Datum, TD, which is 100 m below Ordnance Datum

[*] Stiffness of the Woolwich Clays and the Chalk increases linearly from the minimum at the top of the stratum to the maximum at the base of the stratum.

[#] (h) and (v) indicate stiffnesses and permeabilities in the horizontal and vertical directions respectively.

Table 2.3 *Summary of construction sequence at Canada Water*

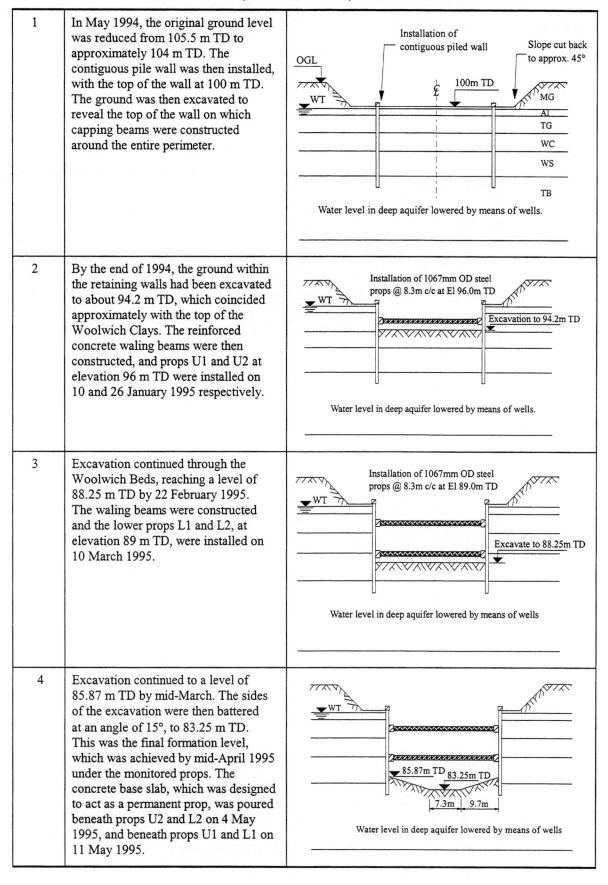

1	In May 1994, the original ground level was reduced from 105.5 m TD to approximately 104 m TD. The contiguous pile wall was then installed, with the top of the wall at 100 m TD. The ground was then excavated to reveal the top of the wall on which capping beams were constructed around the entire perimeter.
2	By the end of 1994, the ground within the retaining walls had been excavated to about 94.2 m TD, which coincided approximately with the top of the Woolwich Clays. The reinforced concrete waling beams were then constructed, and props U1 and U2 at elevation 96 m TD were installed on 10 and 26 January 1995 respectively.
3	Excavation continued through the Woolwich Beds, reaching a level of 88.25 m TD by 22 February 1995. The waling beams were constructed and the lower props L1 and L2, at elevation 89 m TD, were installed on 10 March 1995.
4	Excavation continued to a level of 85.87 m TD by mid-March. The sides of the excavation were then battered at an angle of 15°, to 83.25 m TD. This was the final formation level, which was achieved by mid-April 1995 under the monitored props. The concrete base slab, which was designed to act as a permanent prop, was poured beneath props U2 and L2 on 4 May 1995, and beneath props U1 and L1 on 11 May 1995.

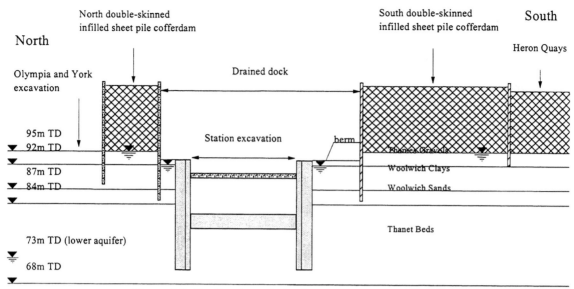

Figure 2.3 *Section through the Canary Wharf site showing cofferdams, excavation and aquifer groundwater levels after dewatering*

2.2.2 Groundwater conditions

The groundwater level in the upper aquifer is influenced by the water level in Canary Wharf dock, which is generally maintained at approximately 104 m TD. As at Canada Water, the Woolwich Clays separate the upper aquifer from a lower aquifer comprising the Chalk, the Thanet Beds and the Woolwich Sands.

Throughout the construction period, deep wells were used to lower the piezometric level in the lower aquifer and then maintain it at approximately 73 m TD. The groundwater level in the upper aquifer within the drained dock (Figure 2.3) was lowered to approximately 92 m TD before excavation between the diaphragm walls. Within the cofferdams, the upper aquifer groundwater level was maintained at approximately 95 m TD by pumping from a system of shallow wells. The two different piezometric levels were separated by the sheet-pile cofferdam walls, which extended into the relatively impermeable Woolwich Clays to provide a cut-off.

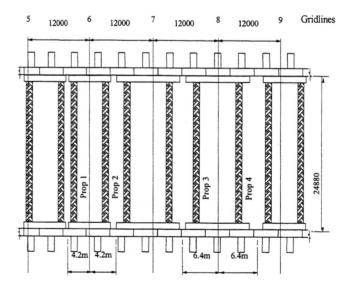

Figure 2.4 *Plan of excavation showing location of monitored props at Canary Wharf*

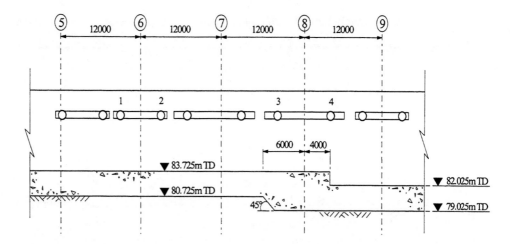

Figure 2.5 *Section through excavation showing details of base slab at Canary Wharf*

2.2.3 Construction details

The sides of the 24.88 m wide station box were formed from diaphragm walls consisting of 4.5m wide × 1.2 m thick × 22 m deep T-panels, supported by a single row of temporary props at a level of 90.5 m TD. The props were 1220 mm diameter × 15.4 mm thick tubular steel sections and spanned 22.74 m between twin 914 mm I-beam walings. The props were not installed at a uniform spacing along the excavation, but were spaced in pairs either 6 m apart (on an 8 m waling) or 8m apart (on a 12 m waling). Four props (numbers 1, 2, 3 and 4) were monitored. Props 1 and 2 were installed at 6 m centres, each supporting a length of wall of approximately 4.2 m; and props 3 and 4 were at 8 m centres, each supporting a length of wall of approximately 6.4 m (Figure 2.4).

The formation level and base slab thickness varied along the length of the excavation, as indicated in Figure 2.5. The sequence of excavation, installation of the temporary props and construction of the permanent concrete base slab prop is summarised in Table 2.4.

2.3 INSTRUMENTATION

Vibrating wire strain gauges (Geokon type VK-4101), incorporating thermistors, were installed (four at each end) on four props in each excavation. Strain gauge and temperature readings using a multi-channel data-logger (Campbell Scientific model CR10) were taken every two hours – as far as practicable – throughout the entire period that the temporary props were in place, giving an essentially continuous record. Inclinometer tubes, installed in the retaining walls near to the ends of the instrumented props, enabled deflected profiles of the walls to be measured by hand at intervals. Pore water pressures were measured, using the piezometers installed for construction monitoring purposes.

The four gauges at each end of each instrumented prop were located at the quarter-points of the cross section (ie at the 3, 6, 9 and 12 o'clock positions) so that bending about the horizontal and vertical axes, as well as the axial load, could be investigated. The gauges were installed approximately 1500 mm from the ends of the props, which was at the time considered to be far enough from the waling beam for load redistribution over the cross section to have occurred.

Table 2.4 *Summary of construction sequence at Canary Wharf (continued on next page)*

1	

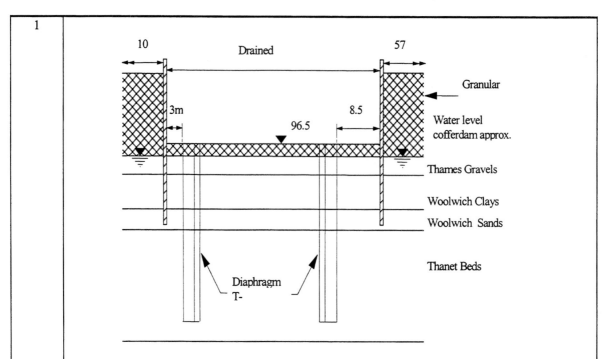

Work on the new JLE station started with the reclamation of the dock, which involved the installation of the south double-skinned sheet pile cofferdam. The sheet pile cofferdam walls extended into the relatively impermeable Woolwich Clays, providing a pore water cut-off. The dock was dewatered during April 1994, after which the dock silt was removed. Within the drained dock, a working platform was provided by a layer of granular fill to a level of 96.5 m TD. The cofferdam was infilled with granular fill to about 106.5 m TD. Reclamation was completed in June 1994. The level of the upper aquifer within the drained dock was lowered to 92 m TD. The lower aquifer level was lowered across the site to 73 m TD over a period of approximately six months.

2	

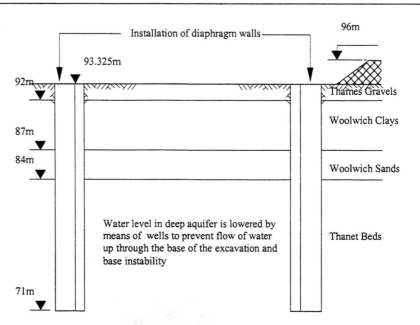

The diaphragm walls were installed within the station excavation. This started in September 1994 and was completed by the beginning of August 1995. Generally, it took 1.5 days to excavate the trench for each T-panel under bentonite slurry. Each excavation was left standing for approximately 12 hours before concreting, which took about 12 hours. The tops of the diaphragm walls were gradually reduced over the following months to 93.325 m TD. A berm approximately 2.7 m high was left in place on the south side of the excavation in order to stabilise the cofferdam wall.

3	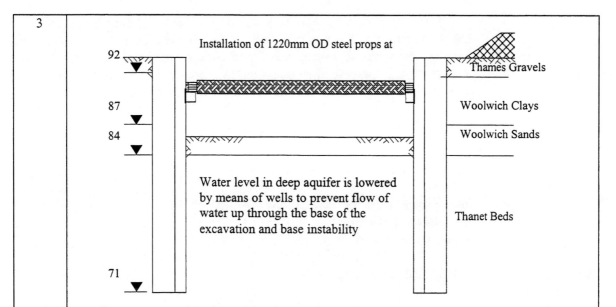

Installation of 1220mm OD steel props at

92 — Thames Gravels
87 — Woolwich Clays
84 — Woolwich Sands

Water level in deep aquifer is lowered by means of wells to prevent flow of water up through the base of the excavation and base instability

Thanet Beds

71

Excavation between the diaphragm walls started in mid-August 1995 at the west end of the station box. By the beginning of September 1995, the excavation had reached approximately 86 m TD. The temporary props between gridlines 1 and 9 were installed during the first two weeks of September 1995. Props 1 and 2 were installed on 8 September 1995 and props 3 and 4 were installed on 14 September 1995.

4	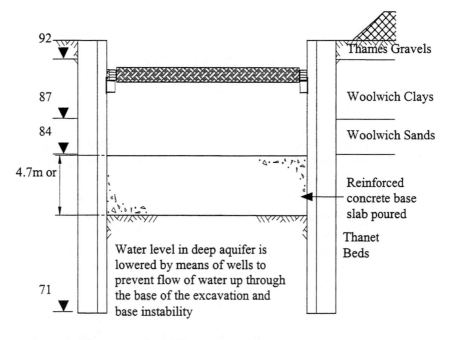

92 — Thames Gravels
87 — Woolwich Clays
84 — Woolwich Sands

4.7m or

Reinforced concrete base slab poured

Thanet Beds

Water level in deep aquifer is lowered by means of wells to prevent flow of water up through the base of the excavation and base instability

71

Excavation then proceeded to the formation levels of 80.725 m and 79.025 m TD, which in the research area were reached by the end of September 1995 and mid October 1995 respectively. The concrete base slab was poured on the following days:

gridline 5.5–6	(prop 1)	15 Nov 1995
gridline 6–6.5	(prop 2)	17 Nov 1995
gridline 6.5–7.2		21 Nov 1995
gridline 7.2–7.6	(prop 3)	23 Nov 1995
gridline 7.6–8.3	(prop3/4)	28 Nov 1995
gridline 8.3–9	(prop 4)	30 Nov 1995

The results later indicated that this may not have been the case, particularly (as at Canary Wharf) where the end detail results in a highly non-uniform distribution of stress over the cross-section of the prop. Subsequent investigation showed, however, that the average reading of three or more gauges equally spaced around the circumference does give an accurate indication of the axial load in the prop (Batten *et al*, under review).

2.4 ANALYSES AND DESIGN CALCULATIONS

The field results were compared with finite element analyses, limit equilibrium analyses, and the original design calculations. For Canada Water, the measured prop loads were also compared to loads calculated using WALLAP and the new distributed prop load method described in CIRIA publication C517, *Temporary propping of deep excavations – guidance on design* (1999).

2.4.1 Finite element analyses

A series of plane-strain finite element analyses was carried out for each site using the program CRISP (Britto and Gunn, 1987), to investigate the sensitivity of the temporary prop loads to changes in the soil parameters and input assumptions. The soils were modelled as elastic/Mohr-Coulomb plastic materials, and construction activities were represented as closely as possible. At Canary Wharf, the analyses included modelling the draining of the dock, dewatering of the upper and lower aquifers, construction of the cofferdams and installation of the diaphragm walls.

At Canada Water, the idealised geometry of the cross-section through the excavation was symmetrical about the centreline, thus the finite element mesh only needed to represent one half of the excavation. At Canary Wharf, however, the geometry of the cross-section was not symmetrical and the entire excavation had to be modelled in the analyses.

The concrete of the walls and base slabs was modelled as an impermeable linear elastic material with a Young's modulus (E) of 22×10^6 kN/m^2, a unit weight (γ) of 24 kN/m^3 and a Poisson's ratio of 0.15. In the analyses for both sites, the wall was assumed to be of a uniform thickness, with the same bending stiffness per metre run (EI) as the contiguous pile or T-panel diaphragm walls used in reality.

It is commonly recognised that the process of wall installation will alter the *in-situ* stress state of the soil, resulting in a pre-excavation lateral earth pressure coefficient (K_i) which is different from the *in-situ* value (K_0). The magnitude of these stress changes will depend on the method of wall installation and the way in which the ground is supported prior to concreting. During installation of the piles at Canada Water, the ground was supported by a temporary casing to the base of the Thames Gravels, below which a bentonite slurry support was used. The effects of wall installation at Canada Water were investigated by means of a separate axisymmetric finite element analysis, which simulated the installation of a single pile. Removal of the pile casing may have caused a loosening of the Thames Gravels. Wall installation effects in this stratum were therefore modelled by using a Young's modulus close to the lower end of the range given in Table 2.1 of 20 MN/m^3. (A finite element analysis carried out with a Young's modulus of the Thames Gravels of 50 MN/m^3, but all the other factors the same, led to an increase in the calculated upper prop load of approximately 10 per cent; the lower prop load was not significantly affected.) The diaphragm walls at Canary Wharf were constructed entirely under bentonite slurry. Modelling of the wall installation process in this case was included in the main plane-strain analyses, but separate axisymmetric analyses were also carried out in order to provide a comparison.

2.4.2   Limit equilibrium analyses

Limit equilibrium analyses were carried out for the walls at both sites in terms of effective stresses, assuming pore water pressures in equilibrium with the conditions imposed by the dewatering system (Figures 2.6a, b and c). In order to take into account the effects of wall installation, the initial earth pressure coefficients (K_i) were assumed to be equal to 1 in all soil strata, both in front of and behind the wall. As the depth of excavation was increased, rotational equilibrium was maintained by reducing K_i towards the active limit K_a in the retained soil, maintaining a uniform strength mobilisation factor M (where $\phi'_{mob} = \tan^{-1}[\tan\phi'_{crit}/M]$) in all of the strata behind the wall. In front of the wall, the earth pressure coefficients were kept at the assumed pre-excavation values until the soils behind the wall had reached fully active conditions.

As further excavation continued, equilibrium was satisfied by increasing the earth pressure coefficients (and hence the mobilised strengths) in the soil in front of the wall. The same strength mobilisation factor M was assumed to apply in all of the strata in front of the wall. The earth pressure coefficients K_a and K_p were taken from Caquot and Kerisel (1948), assuming a soil/wall friction angle δ equal to the mobilised soil strength ϕ'_{mob}.

Following placement of the lower level props at Canada Water, the system becomes statically indeterminate, and the rate of mobilisation of soil strength with increasing excavation depth was assumed to remain constant.

At Canary Wharf, separate calculations had to be carried out for the north and south diaphragm walls because the geometry of the excavation and its surroundings was not symmetrical. The surcharge due to the north cofferdam was modelled as a strip load, using the method suggested by Pappin *et al* (1986). The south cofferdam was taken into account by calculating the lateral load on the diaphragm wall resulting from the pressures required to maintain equilibrium of the cofferdam sheetpile wall, behind which fully active conditions were assumed to have been reached (Figure 2.6b).

2.4.3   Design analyses

The temporary prop loads for Canada Water were calculated at the design stage using WALLAP, which is a simplified soil-structure interaction analysis program. The design prop loads for Canary Wharf were originally calculated using WALLAP, but subsequently higher values were calculated using the finite element program SAFE. Design loads are given in Tables 3.1 and 3.2.

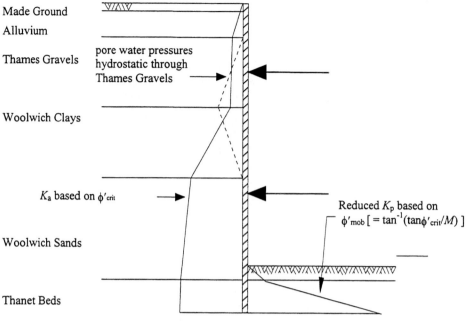

Made Ground
Alluvium

Thames Gravels

pore water pressures
hydrostatic through
Thames Gravels

Woolwich Clays

K_a based on ϕ'_{crit}

Reduced K_p based on
$\phi'_{mob} [= \tan^{-1}(\tan\phi'_{crit}/M)]$

Woolwich Sands

Thanet Beds

Fully mobilised active pressures   *Less than passive pressures*

Figure 2.6 *Assumed stress distributions for limit equilibrium calculations*
(a) Canada Water

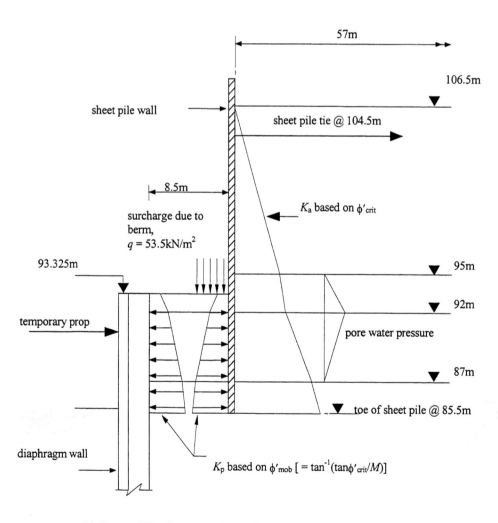

57m

106.5m

sheet pile wall

sheet pile tie @ 104.5m

8.5m

K_a based on ϕ'_{crit}

surcharge due to
berm,
$q = 53.5 kN/m^2$

93.325m

95m

92m

temporary prop

pore water pressure

87m

toe of sheet pile @ 85.5m

diaphragm wall

K_p based on $\phi'_{mob} [= \tan^{-1}(\tan\phi'_{crit}/M)]$

(b) Canary Wharf – south side cofferdam

CIRIA PR77

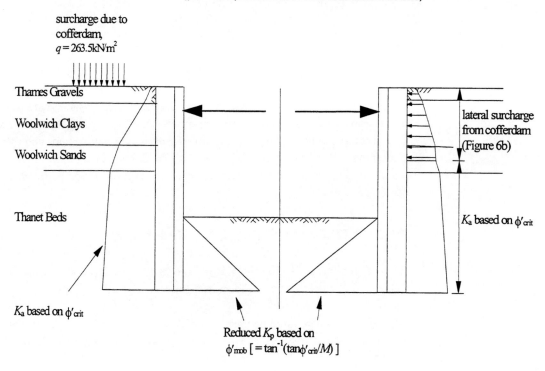

North   South

(pore water pressure behind both walls taken to be zero)

surcharge due to
cofferdam,
$q = 263.5 kN/m^2$

Thames Gravels

Woolwich Clays

Woolwich Sands

Thanet Beds

lateral surcharge
from cofferdam
(Figure 6b)

K_a based on ϕ'_{crit}

K_a based on ϕ'_{crit}

Reduced K_p based on
$\phi'_{mob} [= \tan^{-1}(\tan\phi'_{crit}/M)]$

Figure 2.6 *Assumed stress distributions for limit equilibrium calculations (continued)
(c) Canary Wharf – north and south diaphragm walls*

3 Principal results and findings

The main result of the project has been the generation of two high-quality case records of prop loads in large braced excavations, which have formed the basis of an assessment of the suitability of various assumptions and methods of analysis that are used in design. The research has also clarified some important issues concerning the way in which prop loads are monitored (eg for a design using the observational method) and the effects of temperature and certain construction details. The principal results and findings are summarised in this section. Detailed evidence and arguments can be found in the papers listed in Section 6.

3.1 PROP LOADS AND WALL MOVEMENTS

The prop loads (calculated using the average strain in each prop) measured at Canary Wharf and Canada Water are shown in Figures 3.1 and 3.2.

The effects of temperature on the prop loads are very significant but can, for the purpose of comparison with the results of analyses, be substantially eliminated from the data by normalising the loads to a reference temperature as described by Powrie and Batten (under review). The temperature-normalised loads are compared in Figures 3.3 and 3.4 with the prop loads calculated using finite element analysis.

The maximum measured and temperature-normalised prop loads are compared in Tables 3.1 and 3.2 with those calculated at the design stage, and with the results of the limit equilibrium and finite element analyses carried out as part of this research.

Table 3.1 *Comparison of measured and calculated prop loads – Canada Water*

		Upper prop (kN)	Lower prop (kN)
	Measured	4750	2400
	Measured (temperature-normalised)	3000	1750
Design loads	Original design analysis	7188	6304
	Original design analysis but with revised pore water pressures	6416	5677
	As above, but with temperature rise modelled	7478	7437
	Finite element analysis	3452	1892
	Limit equilibrium analysis	3685	1779

Table 3.2   *Comparison of measured and calculated prop loads – Canary Wharf*

			Prop 1 (kN)	Prop 2 (kN)	Prop 4 (kN)
	Measured		3710	5950	7540
	Measured (temperature-normalised)		3230	5740	6850
Design loads	Original design analysis		3780	5760	5760
	Original design analysis with an allowance included for temperature and accidental loading		6640	8620	8620
	Finite element analysis		3105	5590	6114
	Limit equilibrium analyses	North	3416	5520	5609
		South	3980	6323	6395

The inclinometer datums were not established until a significant amount of excavation between the retaining walls had occurred, particularly at Canary Wharf where the excavation had almost reached formation level. The measured wall movements are compared with those calculated (from the time the datums were established) using finite element analysis in Figures 3.5 and 3.6.

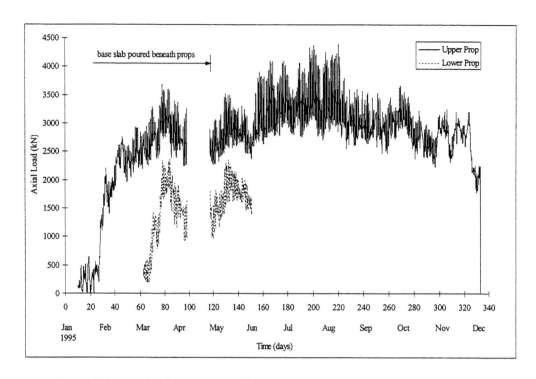

Figure 3.1 *Prop loads measured at Canada Water*

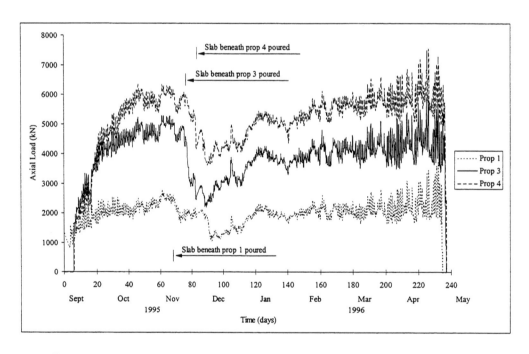

Figure 3.2 *Prop loads measured at Canary Wharf*

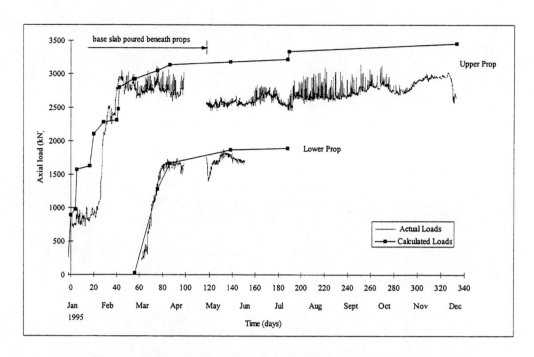

Figure 3.3 *Comparison of measured and calculated prop loads at Canada Water*

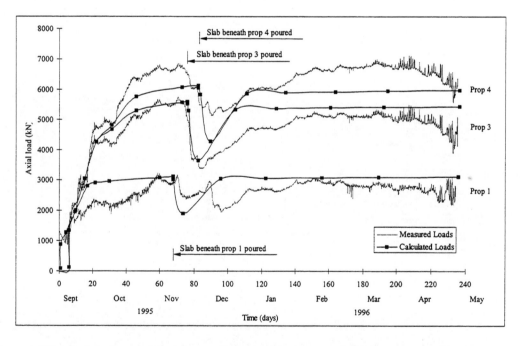

Figure 3.4 *Comparison of measured and calculated prop loads at Canary Wharf*

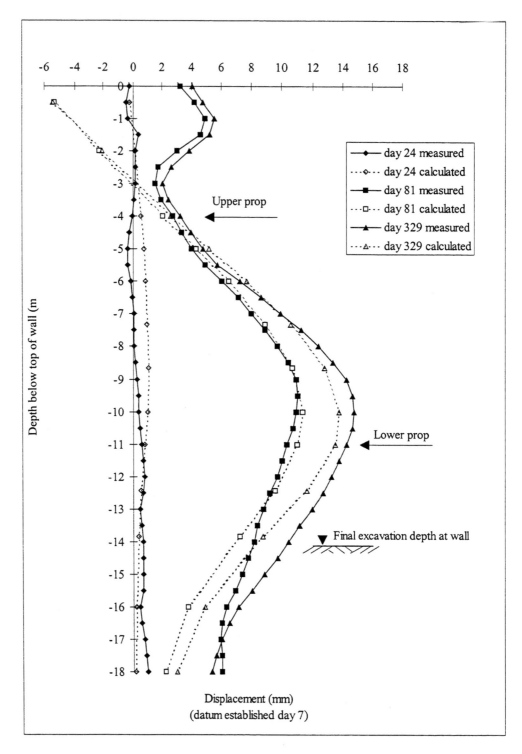

Figure 3.5 *Comparison of measured and calculated wall movements – Canada Water*

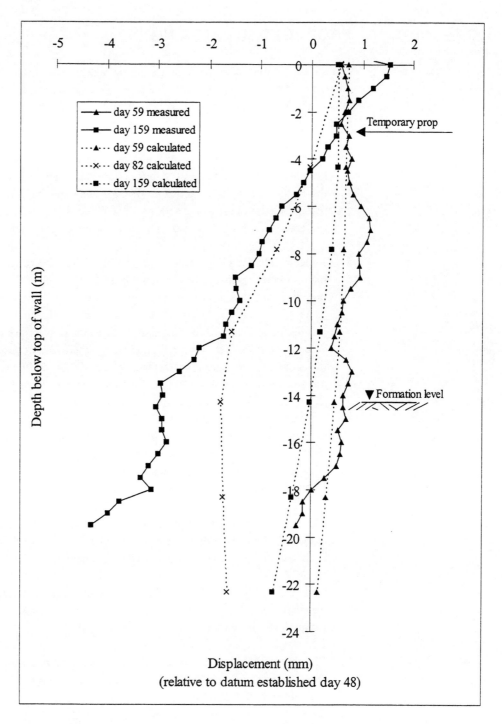

Figure 3.6 *Comparison of measured and calculated wall movements – Canary Wharf*

3.2 PROP LOAD MONITORING

The use of vibrating wire strain gauges for monitoring prop loads is discussed in detail by Batten *et al* (1999). From the experience gained at Canada Water and Canary Wharf, the following recommendations are made for the achievement of accurate and reliable results.

1. Prop temperatures, in addition to strains, should be measured so that variations in prop load caused by changes in temperature can be identified. The possibility of a discrepancy between the actual prop temperature and that recorded by a thermistor incorporated into the gauge sensor can be reduced by painting the prop white, or preferably attaching a thermocouple to the prop itself at the location of each gauge.

2. Reliable datum readings have to be established for each gauge before the prop begins to take up load. Ideally, these datum readings should be checked when the prop is de-stressed prior to its removal.

3. It is desirable to record the strains and temperatures at frequent intervals using an automatic data logger. This facilitates the establishment of reliable datum readings, the elimination of readings affected by external noise and vibration, and the identification of variations in load from temperature changes.

4. As there is the possibility of non-uniform stress distribution in the prop, sufficient gauges are required to calculate the average axial stress accurately and reliably. At least three gauges are necessary for this purpose, but the use of four gauges spaced equally around the circumference of the prop at the 3, 6, 9 and 12 o'clock positions is recommended due to the other advantages of this arrangement (see point 5).

5. The installation of four gauges spaced equally around the circumference of the prop at the 3, 6, 9 and 12 o'clock positions enables the bending moment about both the horizontal (x–x) and vertical (y–y) axes to be determined.

6. Gauges should be installed away from weld lines formed during the fabrication of the prop. Once datum readings have been established, welding in the vicinity of the gauge should be avoided.

7. The gauges should ideally be protected, eg by means of shields fabricated from angle-section steel or rebar. If possible, more cross-sections should be instrumented than the minimum number required, so that sufficient data are still forthcoming in the event of accidental damage or strain gauge malfunction, and also to give an indication of the likely extent of variations in prop load due to differences in ground conditions and construction sequence effects. In excavations that are propped at more than one level, gauges on props already installed are particularly prone to damage while other props are being lifted into place or removed.

3.3   TEMPERATURE EFFECTS

3.3.1   Influence of temperature on strain gauge readings

It is well known that the tendency of a steel prop to expand when the temperature increases gives rise to a potentially significant additional load. In these circumstances, the strain indicated by a vibrating wire strain gauge will give a true indication of the overall prop load, provided (as is usually the case) that the gauge and the prop have the same coefficient of thermal expansion α. If the gauges and the prop have different coefficients of thermal expansion, the gauge reading should be corrected by subtracting a compression of $(\alpha_p - \alpha_g)\Delta T$ from the measured strain $\Delta\varepsilon_m$, where α_p is the coefficient of thermal expansion of the prop, α_g is the coefficient of thermal expansion of the gauge, and ΔT is the increase in temperature.

3.3.2   Temperature-induced bending

The variations in temperature measured at the different gauge locations at one end of one of the props at Canada Water are shown in Figure 3.7. This shows that the prop was never at a uniform temperature, and that the upper surface was subjected to the greatest temperature range. The resulting differential thermal strains on opposite sides of the prop generated bending moments about both the horizontal and vertical axes. Bending moments about the horizontal axis of the prop might also result from the rotation of the retaining wall, as discussed in Section 3.4. At both Canada Water and Canary Wharf, the combined bending moments from temperature and wall rotation were of the same order as the bending moment from the self-weight of the prop.

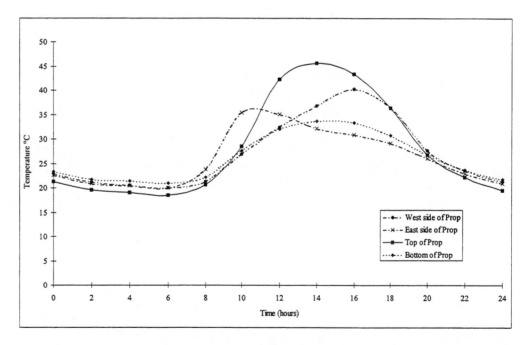

Figure 3.7 *Typical variation in measured prop temperature at Canada Water over a 24-hour period in the summer*

3.3.3 Effectiveness of end restraint

The measured prop loads at both Canada Water and Canary Wharf displayed considerable variation with temperature (see Figures 3.1 and 3.2). The magnitude of any temperature-induced axial load depends not only on the magnitude of the temperature rise, but also on the effectiveness with which the ends of the prop are restrained by the walls they support. The average effective restraint for the props at Canary Wharf and the upper props at Canada Water was approximately 50 per cent (see Table 3.3). However, because of the higher stiffness of the adjacent ground (as shown in Tables 2.1 and 2.2) and the geometry of the support system, the lower props at Canada Water were restrained with a greater average effectiveness of about 65 per cent.

Table 3.3 *Summary of temperature effects on the temporary prop loads at Canada Water and Canary Wharf*

	Prop number	Installation temperature (°C)	Temperature range (°C)	Degree of end restraint (%)	Maximum % of total load resulting from temperature
Canada	U1	4	-3 – +39	52	40
Water	U2	7	-3 – +39	52	43
	L1 and L2	7	1 – +23	65	38
Canary	1	20	-5 – +28	50	20
Wharf	3	20	-5 – +28	50	10
	4	20	-5 – +28	50	7

3.3.4 Adjustment of measured axial loads to remove temperature effects

The relationship between the indicated load and temperature at each gauge location was found to be approximately linear (Figure 3.8), although the gradient of the line was different in each case. By assuming that the relationship between prop load and temperature for a given excavation depth can be idealised as being linear, the measured prop loads may be normalised for temperature effects. This gives an estimate of the prop loads that would have been recorded had excavation been carried out without any change in temperature (Figures 3.3 and 3.4). The temperature-normalised data form a more appropriate basis for comparison with calculated prop loads, which do not usually allow for temperature effects. Note that as the props at Canary Wharf were installed at a relatively high temperature (20°C), the temperature-normalised maximum loads were less than the actual measured values.

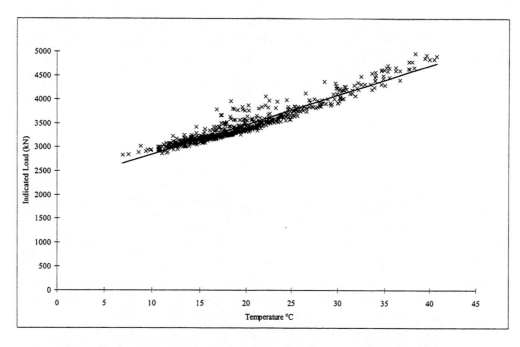

Figure 3.8 *Typical relationship between temperature and load at a constant excavation level and with minimal pore water pressure variation*

3.4   END EFFECTS

The rotation of the wall, an initial lack of fit between the prop and the wall, or the end detail of the prop can all result in significant non-uniformities in the distribution of axial stress over the cross-section, even at some distance (more than three times the diameter) from the end of the prop. At Canary Wharf, the end detail of the props was such that the load was transmitted to the prop primarily through the sides of the cross section (Figure 3.9). Consequently, it was found that at the gauge locations the sides of the props carried, on average, 67 per cent of the total load. The actual distribution of axial load varied for each prop. This was primarily caused by the lack of fit that often occurred between the prop end plate and the waling beam, which resulted in more load being transmitted into one side (and/or the top or bottom edge) of the prop than the other.

A lack of fit at the end of a prop will probably result in larger bending moments. In addition the prop/wall connection will influence the magnitude of any bending moments induced in the props by rotation of the wall. As mentioned in Section 3.3, however, the bending moments measured at Canada Water from the combined effects of wall rotation and differential temperature changes were of the same order of magnitude as those from the self-weight of the prop. Owing to the lack of fit that sometimes occurred at the ends of the props at Canary Wharf, bending moments resulting from wall rotation, differential temperature changes and end effects were up to three times the bending moment due to self-weight. The combined effect of the maximum bending and axial stresses, however, was within the structural capacity of the props.

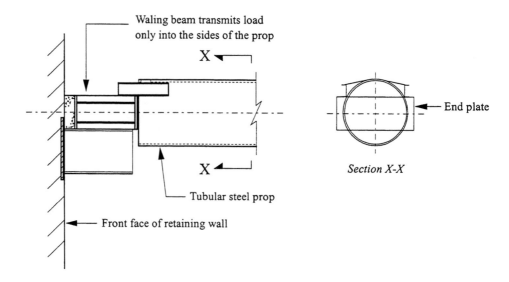

Figure 3.9 *Prop end connection at Canary Wharf (simplified, eg stiffeners on end plate not shown)*

3.5 EFFECTS OF PERMANENT CONCRETE BASE SLAB PLACEMENT

The pouring of the concrete base slab at both Canada Water and Canary Wharf resulted in a reduction in the load in the temporary props (Figures 3.1–3.4). This is considered to have been due primarily to thermal expansion of the concrete base slab which, during hydration of the cement, would have generated a significant axial load in the base slab, in turn causing a reduction in the temporary prop load. The surcharge effect of the slab and the horizontal pressure of the wet concrete on the wall also contributed to the reduction in temporary prop load.

The reduction in temporary prop load following casting of the base slab was most significant at Canary Wharf, where the slab was thickest (Figures 3.2 and 3.4), the reduction in the temporary prop load being approximately 45 per cent. As the concrete hardened, possibly shrinking, there was a gradual partial recovery of the temporary prop loads (by approximately 60 per cent of the lost load for prop 3) over some 30 days. This behaviour was replicated in finite element analyses in which the effects of thermal expansion of the base slab were simulated (Figure 3.4).

3.6 DESIGN CALCULATIONS

3.6.1 Limit equilibrium analyses

Despite the approximate nature of this type of calculation, prop loads close to the measured loads (adjusted for temperature effects) were calculated at both sites (Tables 3.1 and 3.2). At both sites, the soils behind the wall had reached the active condition before the excavation was at formation level, and the earth pressure coefficient in the soil remaining in front of the wall was calculated on the basis of moment equilibrium about the position of the temporary prop. At Canada Water with both the upper and lower props in place, the structure is statically indeterminate and it was assumed that the rate of mobilisation of soil strength in front of the wall with increasing excavation depth remained constant.

At Canada Water, the measured increase in the upper prop load following the removal of the lower prop was apparent in the limit equilibrium analysis. At Canary Wharf, no reduction in prop load following the placement of the base slab was calculated, because the expansion of the base slab due to the hydration of the cement (the main mechanism of prop load change in this case) cannot be modelled in this type of analysis.

It should be noted that the pore water pressures assumed in the analyses for both sites may have been unduly pessimistic as the possibility of negative pore water pressures in the Woolwich Clays was ignored. The satisfactory results of the limit equilibrium analyses may therefore have been the result of some compensating optimism elsewhere in the calculations.

3.6.2   Finite element analyses: Canada Water

Temporary prop loads and wall movements closest to those measured were calculated from the finite element analyses (Figure 3.3), in which:

- the changes in lateral stress due to wall installation were taken into account

- the permeability of the Woolwich Clays was taken as the minimum estimated value, so that negative excess pore water pressure dissipation was only about 35 per cent complete at the end of the modelled construction sequence

- stiffnesses for the Woolwich Clays and the Woolwich Sands at the upper end of the estimated range were chosen

- the soil strength mobilised in the soil remaining in front of the wall (the Thanet Beds) was allowed to exceed the estimated critical state value (but not the estimated peak value).

The calculated prop loads were then about 15 per cent greater than the measured loads, discounting increases in load due to increases in temperature.

A series of parametric analyses, reported in detail by Powrie and Batten (in press), showed the following:

1. In finite element analyses in which wall installation effects were not taken into account, prop loads significantly in excess of those measured were calculated. In the upper props, the calculated loads were 64 per cent greater than those measured, while in the lower props the discrepancy was 54 per cent.

2. When the permeability of the Woolwich Clays was increased so that this stratum was modelled to behave in a substantially drained manner (ie the negative excess pore water pressures induced on excavation dissipated fully during the construction period), loads calculated in the upper and lower props were greater than those measured by approximately 50 per cent and 25 per cent respectively.

3. The use of average – rather than maximum – estimated soil stiffnesses for the Woolwich Clays and the Woolwich Sands resulted in increases in the calculated prop loads of approximately 15 per cent, and an increase in the calculated wall movement following installation of the upper props of about 33 per cent.

4. Limiting the strength mobilised in the Thanet Beds in front of the wall to the estimated critical state value, rather than the estimated peak value, resulted in increases in the calculated loads of 6 per cent in the upper prop and 58 per cent in the lower prop.

3.6.3   Finite element analyses: Canary Wharf

Temporary prop loads and wall movements closest to those measured were calculated in the finite element analyses (Figure 3.4) in which:

- the changes in lateral stress due to wall installation were taken into account

- soil stiffnesses at the lower end of the measured or estimated range were chosen, although a change in soil stiffness did not have a very significant effect on the prop loads

- the soil strength was limited to the critical state value in all strata

- values at the higher end of the range were taken for the permeability of the Woolwich Clays, so that the dissipation of negative excess pore water pressure was complete at the end of the modelled construction sequence

- after the base slab was poured temporary displacement, fixities equal to the thermal strain of the concrete slab were applied to the retaining wall adjacent to the slab.

Overall, the most significant factors for both sites were:

1. The effects of wall installation, which could affect the calculated prop loads by up to 55 per cent.

2. The permeability of the Woolwich Clays, which could affect the calculated prop loads by up to 30 per cent.

Soil stiffnesses were of secondary importance, generally affecting the calculated prop loads by approximately 15 per cent.

The major difference between the assumptions made in the finite element analyses for the two sites was therefore the permeability of the Woolwich Clays. This apparent discrepancy can be explained by a different particle size distribution and/or the removal of most of the overburden from the clays within the dock at Canary Wharf. The reduction in effective stress, and possibly the formation of cracks, would cause the permeability of the Woolwich Clays to increase.

3.6.4   Simplified soil-structure interaction analysis (WALLAP): Canada Water

Prop loads closer to those measured were calculated using the program WALLAP (Table 3.4) (1) by taking a reduced pre-excavation lateral earth pressure coefficient, $K_I = 0.75$, in the Woolwich Clays and Woolwich Sands to allow for the effect of wall installation; (2) by using less conservative pore water pressures; and (3) by removing the assumption of a flooded tension crack behind the wall (Beadman, 1995).

Table 3.4 *Comparison of measured prop loads and those calculated at formation level using WALLAP analysis*

		WALLAP analyses
Prop level	Measured (temperature-normalised)	Reduced K_i and amended pore water pressure
96 m	3000 kN	2573 kN
89 m	1750 kN	2473 kN

3.6.5 Distributed prop load analysis (CIRIA publication C517): Canada Water

The loads calculated using the distributed prop load method were 38 per cent and 87 per cent greater than the temperature-normalised measured loads in the upper and lower props respectively (Table 3.5). Prop loads for Canary Wharf were not calculated using this method because the geometry is complex and the effect of the adjacent cofferdams cannot easily be taken into consideration.

Table 3.5 *Comparison of measured prop loads and those calculated at formation level using distributed prop load analysis*

Prop level	Measured (temperature-normalised)	Distributed prop load analysis
96 m	3000 kN	4137 kN
89 m	1750 kN	3274 kN

4 Significance of results for engineering practice

1. Loads in temporary steel props can be measured satisfactorily using vibrating wire strain gauges. There are some potential pitfalls, however, which can be avoided by following the guidelines given in Section 3.2.

2. Temperature-induced axial loads are significant in props supporting stiff walls installed at low temperature.

3. Bending stresses in temporary props due to differential temperature changes and wall rotation are likely to be of the same order as those due to the self-weight of the prop.

4. In addition to differential thermal bending and wall rotation, non-uniform stress distributions in temporary props can also arise due to the prop end/waling detailing and lack of fit. Although this is probably unlikely to result in failure of a well-detailed propping system, it should be considered in design and has significant implications for the measurement of prop loads, eg when an observational approach to design and construction is adopted. To obtain accurate prop load monitoring data, the procedures given in Section 3.2 should be followed.

5. Finite element analyses can give realistic estimates of actual prop loads, provided that appropriate assumptions are made concerning the effects of wall installation and the extent to which non-equilibrium pore water pressures persist in low-permeability strata during the timescale of construction.

6. For stiff walls propped near the crest, and walls propped at two levels with a shallow depth of embedment, effective stress limit-equilibrium type calculations in which fully active conditions are assumed in the soil behind the wall can also give reasonable results.

5   Principal conclusions

The following conclusions relate to the two case studies at Canada Water and Canary Wharf, both of which involved stiff, reinforced concrete walls in mixed ground. The generality of the conclusions can only be tested by means of further well-documented case studies.

1. Neglecting temperature effects, conventional methods of analysis (limit equilibrium, finite element) are capable of calculating temporary prop loads similar to those measured in the field, provided that appropriate soil parameters and input assumptions are used. In finite element analysis, the key factors identified were the effect of wall installation and the timescale of excess pore water pressure dissipation in low permeability soils. In a limit equilibrium analysis, it may be reasonable to calculate the prop loads on the basis of effective stresses and fully active conditions in the retained soil, together with a conservative estimate of pore water pressures. Although in design a margin of safety is essential to allow for unforeseen events, such as the accidental removal of a prop, the over-prediction of prop loads seems to be the result of a consistently conservative set of design assumptions rather than any flaw in the underlying soil mechanics principles.

2. Temperature-induced axial loads must be expected to be significant in props supporting stiff walls, accounting at Canada Water for up to 40 per cent of the total load carried by both the upper and lower props. These loads can be estimated on the basis of the anticipated temperature rise, the coefficient of thermal expansion of the prop, and the degree of end restraint provided by the wall and the soil behind it. At Canada Water and Canary Wharf, the degree of end restraint for the props near the crest of the wall was approximately 50 per cent. Due to the higher stiffness of the adjacent ground and the geometry of the support system, the low-level props at Canada Water were restrained with an effectiveness of approximately 65 per cent; the range of temperature experienced by the props, however, reduced with depth within the excavation.

3. Bending will, in general, be induced in temporary steel props by the rotation of the wall and/or temperature gradients across the prop. In many cases, these effects will probably be of only secondary importance, with the bending moments induced being of the same order of magnitude as those due to the self-weight of the prop. Stress distributions may, however, be significantly more non-uniform if there is a lack of fit between the prop end and the waling beam.

4. Vibrating wire strain gauges are entirely suitable for the measurement of temporary prop loads, provided that sufficient gauges are used at each cross-section; datum readings are established before any load is applied; readings of strain and temperature are taken frequently and ideally recorded using a data logger; and the gauges are protected from accidental damage.

6   References

Beadman, D R (1995)
Private communication

Britto, A M and Gunn, M J (1987)
Critical state soil mechanics via finite elements
Ellis Horwood, Chichester

Caquot, A and Kerisel, J (1948)
Tables for the calculation of passive pressure, active pressure and bearing capacity of foundations
Gauthier-Villars, Paris

Geotechnical Consulting Group (1991)
Jubilee Line Extension Project, Sectional interpretative report 2, Canada Water to Pioneer Wharf

Glass, P R and Powderham, A J (1994)
Application of the observational method at the Limehouse Link
Geotechnique 44 (4), pp571–776

Marchand, S P (1997). Temporary support to basement excavations and strut load monitoring
Proceedings of the Institution of Civil Engineers (Geotechnical Engineering),
July 1997, pp141–154

Ove Arup and Partners (1991)
Jubilee Line Extension, Sectional interpretative report 3, Isle of Dogs

Pappin, J W, Simpson, B, Felton, P J and Raison, C (1986)
Numerical analysis of flexible retaining walls
Proceedings of a symposium on computer applications in geotechnical engineering
Midland Geotechnical Society, Birmingham

Twine, D and Roscoe, H (1999)
Temporary propping of deep excavations – guidance on design
CIRIA publication C517
Construction Industry Research and Information Association, London

Publications arising directly from this research

Batten, M (1998)
Prop loads in two large excavation
PhD thesis, University of Southampton

Batten, M and Powrie, W (in preparation)
Comparison of measured and calculated prop loads at Canary Wharf station

Batten, M, Powrie, W, Boorman, R, and Yu, H T (1996)
Measurement of prop loads in a large braced excavation during the construction of the
JLE station at Canada Water, East London
Geotechnical aspects of underground construction in soft ground (Mair, R J and
Taylor, R N [eds]), pp57–62
Balkema, Rotterdam

Batten, M, Powrie, W, Boorman, R, and Yu, H T and Leiper, Q (1999)
Use of vibrating wire strain gauges to measure loads in tubular steel props supporting
deep retaining walls
Proceedings of the Institution of Civil Engineers (Geotechnical Engineering),
Vol 37, Issue 1, pp3–13

Powrie, W and Batten, M (in press)
Comparison of measured and calculated prop loads at Canada Water station
Accepted for publication in *Geotechnique*